No Secrets

Nancy White

W9-DDP-101

Fearon
Belmont, California

DOUBLE FASTBACK® ROMANCE Books

Cover illustrator: Terry Hoff

ISBN 0-8224-2381-2
Library of Congress Catalog Card Number: 86-81657
Printed in the United States of America
1. 9 8 7 6 5 4 3 2

"**H**ey, Jill, where did you get this butter?" an unshaven man with a big grin on his face called out to the pretty waitress behind the counter.

"What's the matter with it?" Jill answered. She always let the guys tease her about the food at the Pit Stop. It was everybody's favorite game at the highway restaurant where she'd worked for the past 18 months.

"Tastes like you scraped some of the grease from the walls and put it on my pancakes," the man laughed.

1

Jill grinned at him. "Bernie, I know you don't like your pancakes dry, so I just might have slipped a little extra something on them."

Bernie started clutching at his throat as if he were choking. "Oh, no, not the carburetor fuel again."

The rest of the guys at the counter started to laugh at Bernie. He—and Jill—were two of the things that made the Pit Stop such a popular place along the highway.

"What's going on out there?" a handsome young man with silky-looking brown hair said as he peered out from the kitchen.

Jill waved lightly at her boyfriend. "It's just Bernie again, Ken," she smiled. "You know how much he loves your cooking."

Ken Jacoby frowned and ducked his head back into the kitchen. "Can he do any better, I wonder?" he muttered to Jill.

Jill saw that Ken was a little annoyed. She went over to the window between the kitchen and the restaurant and said, "It's nothing, Ken. You know Bernie likes to kid around." Sometimes she wished her boyfriend weren't so sensitive about the truckers. After all, they were regulars at the restaurant.

"Those guys pay too much attention to you," Ken said with a frown on his face.

Jill put her hands on her hips. "They're only *joking*," she said emphatically.

"They joke too much."

"What do you want?" Now Jill was beginning to get a little annoyed. This wasn't the first time they'd had a discussion like this. "These guys work really hard and relaxing in this place is a chance for them to have a little fun."

"I think they hang around here because of you." Ken's frown deepened.

"Don't be silly. This is the only truck stop between here and Carsonville." She was getting impatient with Ken's jealousy. And this wasn't the first time. "What do you want them to do, grab a sandwich in their trucks?" She stared at Ken. "Then you and I would both be out of a job." She turned to go back to the customers.

"Maybe I'd be, but you wouldn't," Ken said in a soft voice.

"What's that supposed to mean?" But Jill knew very well what he meant.

"You're not going to be here much longer, anyway. . . . Not after you become a fancy court stenographer."

Jill shook her head. "What am I going to do with you?" she said with a smirk.

Ken grinned affectionately at her. "I have a few suggestions I'll tell you about Saturday night," he answered, giving her a playful tap on the arm.

"Come on, Jill," Bernie called. "Bring me a cup of coffee. I want to show the guys how I can stand a spoon up in it." The counter rocked with the guys pounding their fists and laughing at Bernie.

Jill poured him a cup of coffee. She knew that the truckers didn't think Bernie was *that* funny. They just liked to egg him on and see how far he would go. The week before he *had* actually stood a toothpick up in his coffee. But that was only because he had put a small piece of toast in the bottom of his cup.

"So how's that school thing of yours going?" another trucker next to Bernie asked.

"Pretty good," Jill answered.

"What is it you're going to be?" he asked.

Jill looked at him with a smile. She really liked these guys, and she was going to miss them. They were like protective older brothers with her. Though most of them looked as if they could put a guy away with one punch, they were gentle and sweet to Jill. They treated her like a princess. They did joke about the food, but she knew it was all in fun. The Pit Stop was part of a chain of diners dotted all along Route 95. And they all had the same food.

Jill grabbed a plate of toast from the counter and winked at Ken. She wanted to reassure him that he was her number-one guy.

Turning back to the truckers, she said, "In another few months, I'm going to be an official court stenographer."

"Better be careful they don't arrest you first for attempted manslaughter," Bernie grinned.

"Huh?" Jill said.

"Trying to poison people with their breakfast is a serious offense."

Jill gave Bernie a playful shove on the arm. "You guys are too much." As she laughed with everyone else, Jill could feel

Ken's eyes practically piercing the back of her neck.

$$ $$

Jill rubbed her eyes sleepily as she and Ken walked to Ken's car. "I'm really beat. I wish I didn't have class tonight."

"So skip it," Ken said casually.

"I can't do that," she said firmly.

"Sure you can," he pressed. "Instead of dropping you off at school, I'll take you out for some burgers and fries. Then you can go home and get some sleep." He shrugged his shoulders, smiled, and put his arm around her shoulder. "Sounds better than class, right?"

It did sound tempting to Jill. But she had paid a lot of money for this course and she was determined to graduate. She rested her head on Ken's shoulder and sighed. "It does sound nice, but you know how much the course means to me. For one thing, it means a job where I won't have to be on my feet all day."

"I don't mind it," Ken said proudly as he stroked Jill's soft ash-blond hair.

"I'm sure it's OK for some people, but it really tires me out. I'll be much happier in a job where I can sit down."

"Oh, come on, Jill, you just feel like complaining."

"No, really—"

"Besides," Ken went on, interrupting her, "maybe it's standing all day that keeps your legs looking the way they do."

"What do you mean?"

"I don't want them to look anything but fabulous," he said. "My girl should have the best of everything." Then he hugged her.

"You mean *look* the best," Jill answered. Part of her liked the fact that Ken was so possessive with her. He was proud of her and liked showing her off—like a prize he'd won somewhere. But another part of her didn't like the fact that he sometimes treated her as more of a thing than a person. He didn't mean to be that way. Ken had said so himself. He just couldn't help it. But she didn't like feeling that the main reason Ken liked her was that she was pretty.

"What you really mean is, *you* should have the best of everything," Jill corrected him. It came out sounding kind of boastful, but she didn't mean it that way.

They got to Ken's car, a dented old Buick that he loved. He always said it had character and personality, not like the flashy cars that some guys drove. He turned to Jill. "So what'll it be? A burger, fries, and me," he said with a big smile, "or school, steno, and a bunch of grinds?" He finished with a frown.

"We are not grinds," Jill protested.

Both of them slipped into the front seat. Ken poked a tape into the deck he'd rigged into the dashboard. Loud music filled the car.

Jill turned the volume down. "We aren't grinds," she repeated. "Just because I want to have something a little different . . ." She paused for a moment to collect her thoughts. She was sick of Ken's attitude, and she wanted him to understand how important the steno course was to her.

Maybe it was the fact that she was so tired
—but so determined to go to class—that
made her say just what she was thinking.

"Don't you ever dream of doing anything
different?" she asked Ken in a soft voice.

"Why would I want anything different?
What's the matter with the way things are?"
He looked genuinely puzzled as he pulled
out onto the highway.

"It's just that . . . ," Jill hesitated, "well, do
you always want to be doing what you're
doing?"

"Why go through the worry of finding
something different now? It's steady work.
No big hassles, and . . ." He turned to her
with one of the sweetest smiles. "I get to be
with you almost all the time."

Ken's answer wasn't a big surprise to Jill.
She knew that Ken was content with things
the way they were. But that bothered her

because she felt the need to go on to something different. Sure, she wanted the security of a job the way Ken did, but she wanted a different job, something *new*.

Jill was 20 years old and, after 18 months, felt she'd been a waitress long enough. She thought she was too young to settle into anything. The world was full of exciting opportunities. And it was too easy to forget that. She wanted to reach out into the world and see what she could do. Nobody—not even Ken—could make her give that up.

Ken's desire to be with her all the time was another thing that bothered Jill. It seemed as if she and Ken had always been together. They had known each other since ninth grade and had dated on and off ever since then. Now that they worked together, it seemed as if they were practically married. And she was definitely too young for that! Jill really valued her independence. She felt there was too much about herself she didn't know.

The steno class was her first step toward finding out—about herself and the world. It was hard, especially since she had to work all day, but it was exciting. It was new. And she wondered what doors it might open for her.

Suddenly the music blared and Jill was shaken out of her thoughts. She looked over at Ken with a startled face. "What happened?" she asked.

"I turned the music up to get your attention."

Jill rubbed her ears. "Well, you've got it, even though I might not be able to hear what you say."

"So where are you going? School or Jake's for some burgers?"

Jill hesitated when she saw how much it meant to Ken for her to go with him, but her mind was made up. "School," she sighed.

Ken pulled up in front of the Perkins School. "Sure you don't want to change your mind?"

Jill leaned over and kissed him on the cheek. "No, but thanks anyway."

"Want me to pick you up later?"

Jill ruffled his hair. "No, thanks. I'll take the bus home."

"It's no problem," he insisted.

Jill was beginning to feel slightly trapped. "No, I'm fine," she said and stepped out onto the sidewalk. She turned and watched

Ken drive away, almost afraid that he'd circle the block and come back for her. He never seemed to want her out of his sight.

"Pizza Prep," Jill smiled to herself as she walked up the stairs of the Perkins School. She always called it that because she'd first seen the ad for the course on the bulletin board at her favorite pizza parlor. She had copied down the phone number, and it had lain on her bedside table for two weeks. Finally, she'd called the number and enrolled in the course.

That had given her a good feeling. She'd felt the same way when she'd quit her job at Woolworth's to take the job at the Pit Stop. The job at Woolworth's had been her first, and she'd worked there all through high school. But after years of counting inventory, she'd yearned for something new.

So, not long after she graduated from high school, she switched jobs. Two months later Ken got a job at the Pit Stop, too.

Now she was looking for something different again. And the steno course was her ticket. It would take her 12 long weeks and she had to spend a lot of time studying, but she knew it would be worth it.

Jill entered the building and made her way to the classroom. Everyone was just getting settled, so she found her seat and got ready for class. Mr. Brock, the teacher, stood with his eyes fixed on the class, as if to stare them into silence. Jill couldn't help but smirk.

The class had nicknamed Mr. Brock "Count Brocula" because of his fiery eyes and the way he talked. His European accent and his deep voice really made him sound like Dracula. Jill was sure he did it on purpose. Every night she half-expected him to walk into class wearing a cape.

The count waited for complete silence and then said slowly, "Good eeevening, class."

"Good evening, Mr. Brock," a few of the real goody-goody types answered back. Most of the students just mumbled a greeting or snickered.

"Psst, Jill," a small dark-haired girl a couple of seats away signaled. She was nodding her head in the direction of a new guy in class.

Jill smiled back at Debby, her best friend in the class, and then looked at the guy.

All of a sudden, Jill felt like crawling into one of the desks and dying. The guy had looked around and caught her staring at him. She scrawled a fast note to Debby.

"What'll I do? He probably thinks I'm the biggest jerk at school, the princess of Perkins twits." She added a P.S. "Who is he, anyway?"

Debby scribbled back, "Maybe he was checking you out. Don't worry, I'm sure he doesn't think you're a twit. In fact, he seemed to think you were pretty cute. Don't know who he is."

All during class Jill had a hard time keeping her eyes off the cute new guy. What was he doing here? How did he enroll in the middle of the course? Did he already have a girlfriend? Did he like blonds? Ash-blonds, she corrected herself in her thoughts.

Jill had a hard time keeping her mind on her work. The count was pretending to be a judge giving a jury instructions. He was really hamming it up tonight. But it wasn't enough to keep her mind from wandering. Jill couldn't wait for the break.

Before she could even get her stuff together, the cute guy was strolling toward her. Should she run? "Don't be such a dummy," she said to herself. Jill tried to relax, but she couldn't help feeling surprised at herself. How could she get so carried away by something like this? She felt like a 12-year-old schoolgirl. Then she caught Debby making a funny face and drawing a big heart in the air as she pointed toward the guy.

"Hi," he said casually to Jill.

Jill began to fidget with her bag, pretending she was searching for something in it. What she was searching for was someplace to hide. Finally, she realized how silly she must look. She stopped her fidgeting and looked up to meet his eyes.

"Hi," she answered shyly. Ordinarily, she was pretty friendly with strangers, even guys she thought were cute. But this guy had caught her making a fool of herself, or so she thought.

"What do people do on their breaks around here?" He had a really friendly smile that made Jill feel a lot better. Maybe this wasn't going to be so bad after all.

"We go to the cafeteria," she said. "Actually, it's not really a cafeteria. It's just a bunch of machines with different kinds of snacks in them. Most of the stuff is pretty bad," she added.

Then, as if they'd known each other for a long time, the two strolled out of the classroom together.

Jill stopped after they'd gone a few steps down the hall. "Listen, I've got to explain something."

"What, that Mr. Brock is really a vampire?" he teased.

Jill giggled. "No, but we do call him Count Brocula."

"I can see why. What is it you want to explain?"

"First of all, my name is Jill Burgess, and second—"

"Oh, no," he interrupted.

"What?"

"I forgot to tell you my name, too. It's Doug Stoddard. I'm sorry. Go ahead. I didn't mean to interrupt you."

"Oh . . . well, I just wanted to say that I didn't mean to stare at you in class." Jill couldn't believe she had actually gotten it out. She went on before she lost her nerve. "It's just that . . ."

He smiled and gestured for her to stop. "I know. I've never been in class before."

"Right," Jill agreed. Better to let him think that than the real reason she was staring at him. She sighed as they continued on down the hall. Somehow this handsome stranger made her feel both nervous and excited.

Someone was practically having a fist-fight with a soda machine when Jill and Doug arrived at the cafeteria. One guy was playing his tape player at full volume. "Cool it," someone shouted. "This isn't the Rock Stand." The Rock Stand was the name of a local dance hangout.

"Do you want anything to eat?"

"No, thanks. I work at a restaurant all day, and somehow it sort of kills your appetite."

He laughed, and Jill noticed how his eyes crinkled at the edges. He was definitely a good-looking guy, she decided. "I'm going to have some coffee," he said. "It's been a rough day."

Jill wanted some coffee, too. They took their cups and walked out to sit on the front steps. Sipping her coffee in silence, Jill felt completely at ease. It was hard to believe she'd been nervous a minute ago.

Casually she looked over at her companion. She knew Doug was tall and had blond hair, but now she noticed that his eyes were a pretty shade of green.

"What are you looking at?" Doug asked, meeting her eyes with a grin.

"Oh, nothing," she said, smiling to herself. "So, why did you start in the middle of the course?"

"I was enrolled in the daytime steno class, but I just switched to the day shift at the Morton plant. That's where I work. I didn't want to give up the course, so I transferred to the night class. But I still haven't gotten used to the new hours," he yawned.

"What do you do at the Morton plant?" Jill asked. She figured he must be ambitious because Morton was supposed to be a tough place to work.

"Do you really want to know?" he said with a smile.

"Sure, why not? I always like to know what other people do. It's a way for me to learn new things. Besides, I'm sure it's a lot better than what I do."

Doug took a deep breath. "I stand in front of a conveyor belt for the whole—and I mean whole—day. I check to make sure that the boxes are stapled together correctly."

Jill didn't know what to say. Next to that, her job sounded pretty glamorous. "Sounds pretty tough," she said.

"You don't know what real boredom is until you've counted your millionth stapled corner." He shook his head, laughing.

"Don't you get any breaks?"

"Forty-five minutes for lunch and two coffee breaks, one in the morning and the other in the afternoon." He turned to her. "Forget about me. What about you? What do you do?"

"I'm a waitress at the Pit Stop on Route 95."

"Do you like it?" He seemed to be genuinely curious about her.

"It's OK, but I don't want to do it forever," she said. "That's why I'm in this course. I think it can lead to a lot of opportunities. And I sure could use a bigger paycheck." For some reason she suddenly felt a pang of guilt about Ken and how happy he was working at the restaurant. She also wondered how he'd feel if he could see her chatting with Doug. She didn't have to wonder too much about how jealous he'd be.

Suddenly the bell rang, signaling the end of the break. Jill wished they didn't have to go back to class. She really enjoyed talking to Doug. She wished they could spend more time together. Slowly they got up and started back to the classroom.

Doug yawned again. "I'm really sorry. I'm used to getting up at one in the afternoon."

"That's not so bad," Jill said, trying to sound cheerful.

"It is if you work from eight at night until four in the morning."

The two of them were practically back in the count's classroom when Doug said, "Listen, I'd like to talk to you some more. Could we get together Friday night?"

"That'd be great," Jill answered.

"I'm going to have to go home right after class and crash. I'm really exhausted," Doug said, stifling another yawn. "Would you pass me your address and phone number during class?"

"Sure," she agreed happily.

When she got back to her seat, Jill scribbled two notes. She made sure that Doug got the first one, the one with her address and number on it. She sent the second one to Debby. It read, "I think I'm in love."

Jill heard Ken honk his horn as usual outside her apartment house. Sometimes she wondered how her neighbors liked the sound of Ken's horn at seven in the morning. It was only a few short toots, but it was enough to wake up anybody who wanted to sleep a little longer.

"So, are you sorry you went to school last night?" he asked cheerfully when she got into the car.

One of the things that Jill liked about Ken was that he was never really in a bad mood. He wasn't even grouchy early in the morning. Of course, his jealousy and possessiveness were another matter.

"No. It was fine," she answered, making one of the biggest understatements of the year. How could she ever tell Ken about Doug? Jill was too confused to have any answers.

"Are you all set for the boat show on Friday?" he asked cheerfully.

Jill froze for a second. She had forgotten all about it. What was she going to do? She just couldn't give up her date with Doug.

Ken looked over at her. "Earth calling Jill. Earth calling Jill. Boat show Friday," he said in an outer space sort of voice that would have been funny any other time. Still frozen, Jill knew she had to say something. Finally, she did.

"I . . . I can't go," she stammered.

"Why not?" Ken whined. "It was all set."

Jill hated it when Ken whined. It wasn't really a whine, but it was pretty close to it. She was angry at herself, so she got angry at Ken. "Look, Ken, I'm really sorry," she snapped, "but I've got to practice my steno. I've got an important exam coming up."

"OK, OK, we can go on Saturday," he said. They drove the rest of the way to the Pit Stop in silence. Jill felt guilty all the way there.

All during the day Jill's thoughts swirled around in her head. She knew if she told Ken about Doug, he would act as if she'd stabbed him in the back. Just because they hung around together all the time didn't mean they were married, she thought. They weren't even engaged. Maybe she was

ready for a change in this part of her life,
too. . . .

Jill felt nervous as she waited for Doug
on her front porch. He was a few minutes
late, and she wondered if he would show
up. As she waited, she kept glancing around
at the bushes, half-thinking Ken would
jump out and catch her with Doug.

"Doug isn't even here yet," she told herself. But Jill's nervousness remained. She
felt guilty about doing something behind
Ken's back, and there was nothing she
could do about it. She tried to relax. But the
more she tried to forget Ken, the guiltier
she felt.

Finally a car pulled up to the curb. The
window rolled down, and Jill could see
Doug's face smiling out at her. "Hop in," he
said.

Once in the car, Jill felt a lot better. Doug's warm greeting seemed to take half her nervousness away.

"So where are we going?" she asked.

"Oh, I've got a little place in mind. . . ."

"Come on, Doug, where? I'm curious."

"You'll see," he resisted. "It will be more fun if it's a surprise." Doug glanced over and saw the pleading look in her eyes. He sighed. "OK, all I'll say is that it's off-beat, hypnotic, and magical." He glanced over again and smiled when he saw that she was *really* curious now.

"Doug . . ."

"Nope. Not another word." He drove on in stubborn silence, smiling all the way.

"Oh, all right," she gave in. "This had better be good."

An hour later Jill was once again sitting in the front seat of Doug's car.

"I didn't even know we had a magic shop in town," she said happily. In her hand she cradled a soft, furry mouse. She slipped it over her finger and wiggled it around so that it looked as if she were holding a real mouse.

"Do you like it?" Doug said with a grin.

"Sure. It's cute."

"What's its name?"

"How about Doug?" Jill grinned.

"Thanks a lot," he said as he steered into Joe's Burger House.

The two of them sat in a booth and talked quietly as Jill stroked the toy mouse.

When the waitress came over to take their order, she glared at Jill and said, "How dare you bring that disgusting thing in here?"

At first Jill didn't know what she was talking about. Then she followed the woman's gaze to the mouse and laughed. She stroked him a few more times and then took him off her finger. The waitress looked as if she didn't like being fooled. She took their orders and left without a word.

"What would you do if one of your customers surprised you with one of those things?" Doug nodded toward the mouse.

"I'd probably never get a chance to do anything," she smiled. "The truckers would take care of it. They treat me like a daughter or a younger sister—they're awfully nice to me." Jill realized she was leaving out a big part of her life at the Pit Stop by not mentioning Ken. But she figured that Doug would never see her again if he knew about Ken. She just couldn't tell him.

"I have an idea for next Friday or Saturday," Doug offered.

"What is it?"

"The planetarium is having a special light show. Have you ever been to one?" he asked.

Jill had only been inside the planetarium once in her life—in the third grade. And she had never seen anything like a light show. "I haven't," she answered. "But I'd love to go."

"How about Friday, then?"

"That's fine with me."

After Doug took her home, Jill wondered what she was going to say to Ken about next weekend. No matter what she said, she knew there was going to be trouble. And she was right.

"I don't understand why you have to study again on Friday," Ken complained.

"Look, I can't flunk this course," Jill protested, her guilt making her feel angry.

Once again she was lying to Ken about her plans. It didn't make her feel good, but she couldn't help it. She just couldn't face telling either man about the other.

"You didn't always have to study this hard," he said. "You got a crush on your teacher or something?"

Jill felt a pang. Did he suspect anything about Doug? She decided he didn't. It was just his jealousy acting up again. "Don't be silly. If you saw my teacher, you'd laugh."

The show at the planetarium was beautiful. Jill felt as if she and Doug had taken a private trip among the stars.

"Like it?" he leaned over and whispered to her during a simulation of a comet blazing across the night sky.

"I love it," she answered breathlessly. Then she felt his hand slip softly around the back of her neck. It rested gently there for the rest of the show. She thought she was in heaven.

After the show, Jill didn't feel like going right home. Impressions of the night sky lingered pleasantly in her memory, and she didn't want the night to end. Jill looked over at Doug and put her arm around his waist.

"What do you say we walk around the natural history museum for a while?" she said. "After all, it's right here in the building, and it stays open late on Fridays."

"Not tired yet, huh?"

"Nope. How about you?"

"Not after *that* show," he answered.

"So, you want to do it?"

"Sure. It sounds like fun."

When they got into the museum, Jill realized they were practically alone. She could see only a few other people wandering around. Jill was glad for the privacy. Maybe now they could get to know each other a little better.

Doug stopped abruptly at a case of beautiful seashells. After gazing at them for a minute, he said, "I've never seen so many exotic shells in my life."

Jill noticed a glint in his eyes she'd never seen before. It made him look so alive, she thought. And it made her feel more alive, too—just by being with him. "They are beautiful, aren't they?"

Doug looked up without saying anything, and they started walking again.

"You know," he said, "I think working in that plant all day really dulls my mind. All I can think—all I can *feel*—is how boring life is. Does that make sense to you?"

Jill understood all too well what Doug was saying. His words were a part of her, too. "The world is *not* boring, Doug. Sometimes you just have to struggle to see that. I do, too. Besides, what do you think we're studying steno for? So we can get out of our boring jobs."

Doug looked over at her and smiled. "Well, I can't say tonight is boring. And you know who I can thank for that."

"Don't you dare make me blush," she teased. "I don't look good in red."

They both laughed. "I'm about ready to head out into the night air," said Doug. "It's getting kind of stuffy in here. Is that OK with you?"

Jill nodded, and they headed toward the door. Once they were out on the front steps, she took a deep breath. "Doug?"

"Hmmm?"

"If you could have any job in the world, what would it be?"

Doug sighed before he answered. "Oh, I don't know. . . . I've always sort of dreamed of being a lawyer someday, but . . ."

"But what?" Jill urged.

"Well, it's not very realistic," he finished.

"I'll bet you don't know that for sure. How can you limit yourself before you do?"

"Maybe you're right," Doug admitted. "But first I finish steno, right?"

"Right," she laughed.

The couple headed down the front steps. The night air was crisp, and Jill was finally tired. She was looking forward to getting a good night's sleep. She knew her morning would be filled with the memory of an unforgettable evening.

"We're seeing less and less of each other," Ken said. "How much studying do you have to do, anyway?" Before Jill could answer, he continued. "It's not as if you're studying to be a lawyer or anything." He clanked a couple of plates together so loudly that Bernie called out, "Hey, Ken, the food's bad enough in here without getting chunks of china mixed up in it."

Jill didn't feel like arguing. As a matter of fact, she was getting tired of Ken's complaining. So what if they weren't seeing each other as much as they once used to? She wished she could tell him the truth: that she and Doug had a lot in common. She still liked Ken, but he belonged to her past. Doug was part of her present and, she hoped, her future.

When Jill went back to get more orders, Ken gently took her hand and said, "Look, I'm sorry. Can't we at least see each other on Friday?"

Jill felt terrible. She and Doug were already planning to go back to the planetarium. "I can't," she lied. "I've got to go over some of my legal terms and use the machines at school. I've got a lot of practicing to do."

He let go of her hand. "OK," he sighed and went back to work.

It was going to be different from now on, Ken decided as he pulled up in front of the Perkins School on Friday night.

He checked his watch and looked up at the lights blazing in all the windows. "This sure is a hard-working crowd," he thought to himself. He figured that Jill would be coming out in a few minutes. Ken knew that the school closed at nine, so Jill couldn't stay and practice long after that.

Ken checked his watch again. It was 9:20, and most of the windows were now dark. Where was Jill? He began to worry, so he bounded up the steps of the school and found Mr. Brock.

"Have you seen Jill Burgess?" he blurted out to her teacher.

"No. She's not in my class tonight."

"But she came here to practice," Ken persisted.

Mr. Brock shook his head. "No. Students can only practice when classes are not in session, and I had classes for several hours tonight. She wasn't here at all. You must have made a mistake."

"Yeah. I guess so," Ken said and raced to his car. There had to be an explanation. Where could she be?

He decided to go to her apartment and wait outside the building for her. He had to make sure she was all right.

Ken awoke suddenly to the sound of a car pulling up. Bleary eyed, he peered out the window as familiar laughter filled the night air. He couldn't believe his eyes. Jill— *his* Jill—was sitting in a car with some guy he'd never seen before. He leaped out of his car in a flash.

"What's the idea of stealing my girl?" he snarled at Doug as he tore open the car door. "Get out. You've got some explaining to do!"

Doug looked as if he'd been struck by lightning. He turned to Jill. "Who is this guy? What does he mean, 'his' girl?"

Then all three of them were standing on the sidewalk.

"Listen, bub, I've never heard of you, so I don't know anything about 'your' girl." Doug's face had grown flushed with anger.

"I've known her for years," Ken shouted. "She's mine!"

Jill stood helplessly by. Part of her was flattered that two men were fighting over her. Another part—a greater part—was horrified at the result of her lies. Why hadn't she told Doug about Ken? And Ken about Doug?

While Ken was shouting at him, Doug kept looking at Jill for some explanation. But she didn't have any, at least not now. She stood by in helpless silence. Nothing she could say would make any difference now.

Ken finally looked at Jill in disgust. "Studying! I should have known." Then he stormed off to his car, slammed the door, and roared away.

The look on Doug's face was harder to take. He looked more and more hurt as his understanding grew. Finally he shook his head and said, "All along you had a boy-friend. How could you let this happen? How could you be so irresponsible?" Doug got into his car without saying another word. He was still shaking his head as he drove away.

Jill stood alone on the sidewalk, tears streaming down her face. She felt shattered. Too afraid to tell the truth, she had lost everything. And now she was alone.

On Saturday Jill woke up feeling miserable. She had lain awake half the night trying to come to terms with what had happened. Though her mind had raced for hours, she had not been able to think clearly. And she'd finally fallen into a restless sleep.

Now she lay awake in bed watching the sunlight shine through the curtains. She tried to go back to sleep, but she couldn't. The night was over and she had to face the day.

Once she was up, Jill saw that it was already one in the afternoon. She dressed quickly and headed into the kitchen. Maybe breakfast would make her feel better. But halfway through her cereal, she burst into tears.

Jill had never felt so empty and alone. Why had she let this happen to her? Without thinking, she picked up the phone and dialed Doug's number.

"Hello?"

"Doug, this is Jill." She couldn't say any more.

"Jill, I don't know what to say to you, so you're going to have to do the talking."

For a moment, Jill didn't know what to say, either. She just felt like crying. Finally she said, "I . . . I don't know why I did what I did. I know I should have told you about

Ken, but I just couldn't. I'm sorry, and I want to see you. . . . I don't want to be alone. Please . . ."

"No, Jill. I think we both have to be alone for a while. I'm sorry, but I can't see you now." And then he hung up.

Jill walked into the living room and slumped onto the couch. Doug was gone. She had lost him, and it was her own fault. Once again tears streamed down her face.

Jill woke up with a start. Her telephone was ringing. As she reached over from the couch to pick it up, she noticed that it was almost dark outside.

"Hello?" she said sleepily.

"Jill, this is Ken. I want to talk to you."

"Ken, I—"

"I'm willing to forgive you," he said, interrupting her. He sounded almost businesslike, as if he were trying to cover up his feelings. "What you did to me was wrong, but I think we can work it out."

"I want to talk to you, too, Ken. Can I come over?"

"Sure. You want me to pick you up?"

"No. I'll take a cab. See you in about a half hour."

Jill was surprised at herself. Her words had seemed to flow out of her mouth without any effort. And she felt better—as if seeing Ken were the right thing to do.

By the time she reached Ken's apartment, Jill was pretty sure of what she was going to say to him. Ken let her in, and they both settled into living room chairs. Before she could say anything, Ken started talking. "As I said on the phone, I think we can work—"

"Ken, please let me start. I want to try to explain what happened." Jill took a deep breath before she went on. "I'm sorry for what I did. I should have told you about Doug right from the start. But I was afraid. . . ."

"Well, that's over now. I don't want to hear that jerk's name again. That way things can be like they were before."

"No!" Jill said, raising her voice. "I'm deeply sorry for what I did, but I can't go back to the way things were before."

"Oh, I get it. You still want to hang onto that guy. You want me back, too, so you can go on two-timing me?" he snapped.

Jill took another deep breath. "Don't you see?" she said. "It's over between us. It had nothing to do with Doug. It had to do with you and me. We've known each other a long time, but now we want different things in life. That's just the way it had to be."

"No!" Ken screamed, getting to his feet. "I'll get that bum and fix him good. I won't let him take you away from me!"

"I don't belong to you, Ken, and Doug's not taking me away from you. He doesn't want anything more to do with me. Not after what I did. You see, he didn't know about you, either."

"It's still his fault!" Ken raged on.

Jill got up and started toward the door. "Your jealousy isn't going to make this any easier." She opened the door and then turned to face him again. "Good-bye, Ken. Maybe someday we can be friends." Then she closed the door quietly and left.

Jill's stomach was in knots as she approached Mr. Brock's class. She sat in her usual place and searched the room for Doug, but there was no sign of him.

Jill hoped that seeing him in class would not be too awkward. Her day at work with Ken hadn't been easy. She didn't want any more headaches now. She just wanted to finish this course so she could get a new job and get on with her life.

Just before the bell rang, Doug rushed in and took a seat on the other side of the room. He didn't even glance in her direction.

Seeing him was harder than she'd thought. He looked so good, and she longed to be in his arms. Tears started to well up in her eyes, but she fought them back. "I can't start sobbing right here in class," she thought. "Why does he have to mean so much to me?"

Then Mr. Brock swept into the room. He gave his usual, "Good eeevening, class," and launched right into his performance. Despite her mood, Jill couldn't help laughing. But it wasn't long before her attention was once again on Doug Stoddard. She could see him staring blankly toward the front of the room. He looked so far away. "I wonder if he's even thinking about me," she thought.

At the break Doug got up and left the classroom. Jill stayed in her seat. Part of her wanted to run after him, but she knew she couldn't. He had said he didn't want to see her.

When Doug came back, Jill watched him walk to his seat. She still longed for him, but somehow she felt better. Though she was paying for her mistake, she wanted to learn from it and become a better person.

Jill remembered how good it had felt to face Ken with what she'd done. Hard as it was, it had been worth it. She had taken responsibility for her actions.

Jill turned to Mr. Brock and did her best to give him her full attention.

At the end of class Jill stayed in her seat until everyone was gone. Then she slowly walked over to Doug's empty seat. It was her way of saying good-bye to him in her own mind.

Then, shuffling her feet, Jill caught a piece of paper on the heel of her shoe. She reached down and picked it up.

It was a note to her from Doug. "Dear Jill," it said, "I don't know why you did what you did. You should have told me about the other guy in your life. I'm not crazy about all this, but I *am* crazy about you. Please meet me after class to talk."

Jill ran out of the classroom toward the parking lot. She had to catch him. She realized he had probably wanted to give her the note but had changed his mind. They *had* to talk—they just had to. Maybe she hadn't lost him after all.

Once in the parking lot, Jill spotted Doug searching frantically through his books.

Jill went up to him. "Is this what you're looking for?"

Doug's head snapped up in surprise. He gave her an embarrassed grin. "Yeah," he said softly as he pushed her hand gently back. "It is meant for you, but I chickened out. I—"

"Please, I'm the one who should do the explaining. You mean so much to me that I've got to," Jill said, looking into his eyes.

"Go ahead," he nodded.

"I know I should have told you about Ken. But I was afraid you'd never see me again if you knew. It was dumb, and I'm really sorry."

"It really hurt me."

"I know, and I had no right to do that. You were right about what you said that night. I *was* irresponsible. I wanted to change my life, but at the same time I couldn't let go of the past. Making changes always takes courage and strength. I guess I just had to learn that the hard way."

Jill stopped. Her heart was beating furiously. She waited for his answer.

A moment later he took her in his arms. She hugged him as tightly as she could, and his heart beat softly against her ear. That was all she needed. He didn't have to say a word.

The evening was warm as they strolled around town together. Jill no longer felt alone. It seemed that she had the whole world to keep her company. For hours they talked about the future, their dreams, what they hoped for.

As Doug talked happily, Jill wondered what would become of them. Would they always be together? She realized she was being silly. She'd just have to wait and see. Jill turned her attention back to Doug and smiled. For now, this evening was all that mattered.